Abundance For Kids

by

& Ava

Robert N. Jacobs

Grosvenor House
Publishing Limited

The right of Robert N. Jacobs to be identified as the author of this
work has been asserted in accordance with Section 78
of the Copyright, Designs and Patents Act 1988

This book is published by
Grosvenor House Publishing Ltd
Link House
140 The Broadway, Tolworth, Surrey, KT6 7HT.
www.grosvenorhousepublishing.co.uk

A CIP record for this book
is available from the British Library

ISBN 978-1-80381-472-8

"Abundance is not something we acquire. It is something we tune into."

Wayne Dwyer

To my daughter Ava.

You are amazing! You have inspired me
to become a better person and dad.
It is because of you that I wrote
The Abundance for Kids, filled with
lessons and stories of living
an abundant life. I hope these words
will inspire you to live a happy and
fulfilling life. I love you more
than words can say.

Pappa

Index

Index Cont.

Index Cont.

A Letter from the Author

Welcome reader, and thank you for taking the time to open my book. I'm so excited to share with you the wisdom I have gleaned from years of study and exploration on the topic of abundance, and perhaps even more so from being the father of a curious eight-year-old daughter.

In this book, I'll be sharing insights on how children can learn to achieve abundance, no matter what their circumstances or situation in life.

We live in a scarcity mindset world: a world where we focus on what we don't have instead of what we do. In this world, we end up limiting our own potential by believing there's not enough money, not enough opportunity... not enough anything. The Abundance For Kids has been written to show young readers how to move away from this mindset, and how to start living an abundant life.

It's about training your mind and heart to seek out all the resources you need for success, and when you find them, using them to bring more abundance into your life.

I believe that if we empower our children with these tools early on in life, they can begin their journey towards abundance much earlier than those who wait until adulthood to make a change.

It doesn't matter if your child is rich or poor, focused or scattered, thin or overweight... because all kids have the same potential to create abundance. All they need is someone to show them how.

This book provides short stories on practical values for building abundance. This knowledge will also help foster positive habits that will last long after they finish reading the book.

It's my aim that after reading this book, your child will have the strong foundation of confidence, creativity, and courage needed to build abundance at any stage of their life.

So, join me as I begin guiding my own child and your children into discovering the power within them, and learning how to unleash it for maximum success and fulfilment in life.

On: Abundance

Once upon a time, there was a young girl named Rebecca who had a dream to change the world. She knew that for this to be possible, she needed to develop an abundance mindset. But what did this mean?

An abundance mindset for children means recognising that there is enough for everyone. It means understanding that by helping others and sharing our resources, we can make up for any shortfalls. It also means believing in our own power and talents, rather than seeing other people as competition and only seeing the scarcity of everything.

The opposite of having an abundance mindset is a view of the world that leads to feeling insecure. If someone is insecure, they are fearful of others doing well because they believe it must mean they are doing badly. In this mindset, they are always uncertain of themselves.

Rebecca wanted to ensure that her friends and family understood the benefit of having an abundance mindset from an early age, so she set about teaching them all how to embrace it themselves. She explained that it was possible to have plenty without taking away from somebody else's share. She taught them how to recognise their own power, and how developing this attitude would help them later in life when faced with more difficult challenges.

The more Rebecca shared her lessons around abundance with those close to her, the more other people began asking her for advice on how they could develop their own abundance mindsets. Following these conversations, Rebecca realised the incredible potential behind setting an example so that others could learn from it too. This made her passionate about spreading the message far and wide. Not just because it could bring about positive changes in society, but also because she strongly believed in its power herself.

Soon enough, Rebecca had become renowned across the world for teaching people how they could live life with an abundance mindset — something she knew would give them greater success in all areas of their lives both now and in the future.

Ultimately, learning how to have an abundant mindset proved beneficial not only for Rebecca but also for many other people too — fuelling creativity through collaboration rather than competition; creating better outcomes through communication rather than contention; valuing diversity instead of uniformity; and ultimately opening us up to a much brighter future full of hope and opportunity.

The end.

On: Appearance

Once upon a time, there was a young girl named Jennifer. She was always incredibly conscientious about her appearance, no matter what the occasion. She never wanted to look anything but her best, and it showed.

Jen's family could afford the nicest clothes and accessories, but she preferred to keep things neat and simple, yet fashionable. Clean lines and minimal jewellery were the order of the day — nothing too flashy or excessive.

When she was out with her friends, they all noticed how dressed up Jen always looked compared to them, regardless of what she was wearing or how much money she spent on apparel. It wasn't money that made Jen look good so much as it was her commitment to paying attention to details. Her shoes were polished, and her blouse ironed flawlessly, for example.

This kind of attention to detail paid off for Jen in many areas of her life — from school to activities outside of it — because people noticed how well-dressed she was. Whenever possible, even for something as simple as running errands around town or meeting up with friends for lunch, Jen made sure that everything about her outfit looked crisp and presentable: buttons buttoned properly, hems uncreased, and colours coordinated perfectly.

On special occasions where dress codes applied, Jen used these situations as opportunities to show off her sense of fashion style while at the same time still looking elegant and appropriate. People noticed not only how well put together she looked, but also appreciated how sophisticated she looked despite her youthful age — all thanks to dressing smartly.

Jen proved over and over again that you don't have to rely on expensive brand names or logos when it comes down to making an impression. Simply showing commitment by being mindful of what you wear will make people take note in a positive way — especially if you are keen on keeping your wardrobe up to date with the latest trends without going overboard.

After all, looking presentable sends out an important message into this world: it says we are proud to be who we are. So remember, dress sharp; think sharp; live life sharply!

The end.

On: Calmness

Once upon a time there were two close friends. Thomas and Sarah. They were always together no matter what; playing in the park, having picnics or even just doing homework together. One day. Thomas and Sarah were studying for a big test that was coming up. Thomas was feeling very stressed out, and he knew he had to do his best if he wanted to succeed.

When the day of the test came around. Thomas was so nervous that he was almost shaking. But Sarah reminded him to take a few breaths before going into the test, and told him to stay calm and collected no matter what happened.

Thomas took her advice and did his best during the test, but when it was finished he wasn't sure if it went well or not. He couldn't help but feel discouraged because things didn't turn out as well as he'd hoped they would.

Back at home things got even worse when Sarah asked Thomas how the test went. He snapped at her without thinking and started shouting about how upset he was that things hadn't gone his way.

At first Sarah didn't know what to say: she was really taken aback by Thomas's outburst because she'd never seen him act like this before. After a few moments of silence she softly said, "I know you're upset right now, but don't forget that we can still be friends even though things didn't go your way today."

Thomas immediately realised how wrong he had been in losing his temper like that, so he apologised for getting angry and calmed himself down by taking a few more deep breaths.

From then on he vowed never to let his emotions get in the way of being a good friend again. He learnt that although it's okay to feel upset sometimes — especially when things don't work out — it's important to remain calm, collected, and forgiving towards others if we want our relationships with them to last as long as possible.

The end.

On: Courage

Once upon a time there was a young boy who lived in a small village. He had never been brave enough to take on any task, be it an adventure or small chore. Every time he was asked to do something, he would run away and hide from his fears.

One day, the boy heard about an upcoming competition in the town square. Everyone was talking about it and there were rumours that the winner would receive a special prize from the King himself.

The boy decided that he wanted to join this competition and prove his bravery to all his peers. But, when it came to taking the first step towards participating, fear began to creep up inside him.

He began thinking to himself that if he failed, not only would he be embarrassed, he would also be ridiculed by all those around him who were watching. He thought long and hard before finally mustering up enough courage to take part in the competition.

When the day of the competition arrived he was scared beyond belief, yet determined to take part regardless of what happened. He went down to the town square determined not to give in to fear, no matter how much it teased him with its negative thoughts and ideas.

The competition was tough, but with every challenge he overcame, his courage grew stronger and stronger. Eventually, he found himself at the finals – and then he won! He received his reward from the King himself. It was a golden medal for showing such courage when faced with daunting odds.

The young boy learnt an important lesson that day: being courageous is not only beneficial for competitions, but also when you are scared or unsure in everyday life situations like school or work. Courage can help you take chances you may never have even considered before, and guide you through difficult tasks without letting fear dominate your decisions any longer.

For example, at school one day, the young boy got confused during class and didn't understand some of his teacher's lesson. Others were also confused, but they were too afraid to ask about it. The boy decided to put his hand up, even though he was afraid of embarrassing himself, and he told the teacher he didn't understand. This turned out to be very helpful to the others in the class too. Now they could all understand.

From then on, he continued embodying courage in both small and large tasks, which eventually led to him reaching success far beyond what he had ever expected before.

This story teaches us that having courage early on will always benefit us throughout our lives. Whether we need it for something big or small, being courageous allows us to try new things without fear holding us back.

What's more, if we don't learn courage early on then we may not reach our full potential because we let our fears stop us from trying something new, even if we know deep down it could help us grow immensely as individuals.

The end.

On: Curiousness

Once upon a time, there was a young girl named Molly who loved to explore and try new things. She was always asking questions and always curious about the world around her.

One day, she decided to take a chance and try something new: tasting exotic foods from cultures different to her own. She sampled Indian biriyani, Chinese dumplings, and even tried some African okra stew. It was all a very enjoyable and tasty experience.

Molly realised that trying new things wasn't something to be scared of, in fact, it was a lot of fun.

After that, she made it her mission to say yes to every opportunity that came her way. Molly travelled to faraway places such as Japan and Peru, and she tasted every strange dish served up wherever she went.

Her curiosity didn't stop at food. Molly went rock climbing with friends, and even tried Mandarin classes. She also started reaching out to people unlike herself by joining a book club with members from various backgrounds and beliefs. Molly found that getting a glimpse into other cultures and ways of life not only broadened her horizons, but taught her acceptance and tolerance of others. An invaluable lesson for someone so young.

Molly's courage and curiosity opened up a world of possibilities for her, but not everyone is so lucky when it comes to trying new things. Many people are content to stick with their current routines, but without being curious enough to challenge themselves, they risk missing out on possible life-changing opportunities.

Molly knows that without curiosity there is no growth. Without exploration there can be no understanding, and without trying new things there can be no progress or development in our lives.

Molly's story serves as proof that we should never be afraid to step outside of our comfort zones, and that it is so important for us all to stay curious. You never know what exciting adventures await if you do!

The end.

On: De-Cluttering

Once upon a time, there was a young boy named John who had a habit of collecting and hoarding items. Everywhere he went, he would always try to find something to add to his collection. From books, toys, clothes, and more, John loved having lots of things.

At first, it seemed like a fun hobby that gave him joy, but over time his living space became cluttered and overwhelming. Without enough room to move around, John began to feel trapped in his own home. He tried organising the items into piles or boxes but none of it helped make him feel any better.

John soon realised that all the stuff he was hoarding was actually making him feel worse instead of better. The clutter was affecting his mental well-being and preventing him from living a happy life. He needed help in de-cluttering his home and learning how to let go of some of the things he collected.

Luckily, John's friends were able to provide useful advice on de-cluttering and how it could have a positive impact on mental health. John quickly learned about the dangers of hoarding and why it is important to only keep what is truly necessary for day-to-day life. His friends also taught him some solutions for de-cluttering such as donating items that are no longer needed, or finding someone in need who could benefit from what you have in excess.

By following these tips and emptying out some of his collections, John finally felt free from the clutter surrounding him. He even noticed other advantages, such as being able to find items with ease due to the reduced number of possessions in his house. Most importantly, he found that letting go of certain items could lead to more emotional well-being than having them around ever did.

The moral of this story is simple: decluttering can bring many benefits and make life much easier! Don't be afraid to part ways with some unneeded items. Giving away what you don't need can be just as rewarding as buying something new.

The end.

On: Dreaming Big

Once upon a time. there was an ambitious young girl named Jasmine. She had big dreams and a drive to succeed. but she wasn't sure how to make it happen.

One day. when she was feeling especially discouraged. Jasmine heard a wise old man talking about the power of dreaming big.

He told her that dreaming big was not just about envisioning something far-fetched. it was about recognising that every single one of us is capable of achieving great things if we set our minds to it. He said that one way to start dreaming bigger is to set yourself Big Scary Goals.

With enough dedication and hard work. even things that feel impossible at first can be achieved. He advised Jasmine to step outside her comfort zone. because only by doing something different and a little bit "scary" could she discover what she was capable of.

The wise man then said something crucial: *"Jasmine. always remember that you are not average. Whatever your mind can conceive and believe, it can achieve. so think BIG — you have nothing to lose. "*

This made sense to Jasmine. She vowed to take his advice and strive for greatness.

Jasmine quickly realised that as intimidating as it might feel, failure is sometimes just part of winning. She accepted that mistakes are necessary if you want to be successful in your pursuit of greatness, and if you don't make mistakes, your goals are not scary enough! You simply cannot win without failing first.

So, whenever Jasmine felt like giving up, or felt overwhelmed by how difficult the task ahead seemed, she remembered the wise words of the old philosopher: dream big and don't be afraid of failure.

With this newfound motivation and courage, Jasmine worked hard towards achieving her Big Scary Goals until eventually, her wildest aspirations transpired into reality.

The end.

On: Empathy

Once upon a time, there lived a girl who had a kind
and gentle heart. She loved taking care of animals and
helping others who were in need. No matter how hard
things were for her, she always had an understanding and
compassionate attitude towards others.

But what was this special power that she possessed? It
was the power of empathy — the ability to see the world
from someone else's point of view and to understand their
feelings, needs, and wants.

The girl knew that by having empathy, she could bring joy
and harmony into her life as well as the lives of those
around her.

So, what exactly is empathy? Empathy is when we can
truly feel another person's emotions or situation without
projecting our own beliefs onto them. It allows us to
put ourselves in someone else's shoes: to be able to truly
comprehend how they think and why they react in
certain ways.

Empathy is important because it helps us build deeper connections with other people, understand their perspectives better, and find common ground with them instead of getting into conflict.

It also teaches us kindness, and that is something that's greatly needed in today's world.

Being empathetic has many benefits, such as being able to build stronger relationships, and it makes the world a safer place because people are more likely to reach out for help if they know there will be others willing to listen with compassion.

Empathy matters because it gives us insights into our own feelings too. Once we learn how to empathise with others, we become better able to identify our own feelings and reactions, and to be aware of any biases that might get in the way of building true connections.

If you want to become a more empathetic person, start by really listening to what others have to say without judging them or thinking about what your response will be right away. Give them enough time to finish what they are saying and to express themselves wholeheartedly without interruption.

Try putting yourself in someone else's shoes every once in a while. Try thinking like they do before making any decisions or getting into any conversations with them. If you do, you are better able to relate with them on an emotional level, instead of being passive or aggressive most times.

The disadvantages of not being empathetic don't just apply to individuals but to entire communities. It can lead people down a path of misunderstanding one another, which can end up making situations much worse than they already are because of miscommunication or no communication at all.

So, let's take a moment today to think about how we can show more empathy towards those around us — both near and far — knowing that ultimately it benefits everyone involved.

The end.

On: Facing Your Fears

Once upon a time there was a brave little girl named Maria who had many fears. Every day Maria would see something or think of something that scared her. This might be something like seeing a spider or having to speak in front of others.

At times, these fears would seem so overwhelming that she wouldn't even want to leave her house, let alone pursue her dreams. But deep down, Maria knew that she had the strength and courage to overcome them. She just needed to find the strength within herself first.

One day, Maria had had enough of not facing her fears and she decided to do something about it. She made a list of all the things that scared her and slowly started working through them one by one.

First, she faced her fear of spiders by watching documentaries about them. By understanding more about them and how they work, she was able to overcome her fear when one crossed her path.

Next, Maria overcame her fear of public speaking by signing up for speech classes at school and reading books on the subject at home. With practice and guidance from others, Maria began to get more confident in herself. Eventually, she found herself enjoying presentations instead of dreading them like before!

Finally, despite feeling apprehensive, Maria went out into the world and tried new things. She tried cooking, dancing lessons, and even joining a sports team. These activities had once filled her with dread, but finding the courage to face her fears meant she could now grow as an individual and become stronger than ever before.

The more challenges Maria faced and conquered, the happier and more fulfilled she became. She now understood that the only limits she had were the ones in her own imagination. She became so much braver than before and no longer feared the unknown. Instead, she embracing it with bravery and confidence.

Maria showed everyone around her how powerful it can be to you face your fears head on, instead of running away from them — no matter how scary they may seem. In doing so, she felt proud of herself for conquering obstacles, and she now felt quite happy in herself that anything was possible!

The end.

On: Flow

Once upon a time, there was a young boy named Jack who loved to build things. Every day, he would come up with new ideas and build them in his spare time. He built boats and bridges, constructed amazing castles out of blocks and even created a small robot that could walk and talk.

But as much as Jack enjoyed creating these works of art, he felt like something was missing. He often found himself wondering why he wasn't able to focus on his building for very long before becoming distracted by something else.

One day, Jack stumbled upon an old book about the concept of flow. It described how one could become so deeply engaged in their favourite activity that it almost felt like the rest of the world melted away, leaving only them and their project present. Jack was fascinated.

He decided to try it out for himself by focusing exclusively on building projects that made him feel excited and challenged. After a few weeks of practice, Jack managed to get into "the zone" more easily than ever before. The feeling was incredible.

Not only did Jack find it easier to stay focused while working on projects that put him in flow, he noticed other improvements too: he became faster at building things, more creative with his solutions, and sometimes even surprised himself with what he had accomplished. This was because flow allowed him to abandon any expectations around outcome or final product, he could just enjoy the process. He also found that he could take breaks from his projects and things would be clearer in his head, meaning he could come back to them even better than before.

Jack realised that getting into flow meant completely immersing himself in what he loved doing most: creating. This taught him an important lesson. When you focus your energy into the activities you enjoy most, it informs all aspects of life. Your motivation levels increase, your skillset improves quickly, and satisfaction is guaranteed no matter what the end result looks like.

So, the moral of this story is simple: no matter what age you are or how talented you may be, if you want to experience true fulfilment in any activity you do, then make sure it puts you in flow.

The end.

On: Focus

Once upon a time, there was a young boy named Sam. Sam had big dreams and ambitions but found himself struggling to make progress on his tasks. He couldn't seem to focus enough to finish anything. He would always find himself switching between activities, jumping from one task to the next and ending up with nothing ever completed.

One day, while in conversation with his parents, they explained to him why it is so important to focus on one task and give it your undivided attention. "Where Focus Goes, Energy Flows," they said. Sam remembered this phrase and decided that he would try his best to stick with one task and really concentrate on it until it was finished.

He started by picking small tasks that were manageable for him and slowly built up his ability to stay focused for an extended period of time. With each successful completion of a task, Sam felt lighter — like a weight had been lifted from his shoulders. With more energy flowing freely throughout him. he was able to take on bigger challenges that had previously seemed impossible. Every time he persevered. using determination and focus. the reward he gained was immense satisfaction at having achieved something worthwhile.

Sam understood the power of staying focused on a single task. He knew that if he committed all his efforts into completing just one thing. he would do far better than if he tried to juggle many different things all at once. The benefit is not just completing something faster or better. but also feeling much better mentally after achieving success in completing something meaningful. It's this feeling of accomplishment that carries us through the days when we lack motivation or need encouragement.

With this newfound wisdom in mind. Sam never gave up when facing tough tasks. no matter how hard or difficult it got. He simply reminded himself. "Where focus goes energy flows." and continued along his path of success until eventually he found himself achieving many great feats — thanks entirely to focusing all his energy into accomplishing just one goal at a time.

And so the moral of the story is, no matter how large your goals may seem, stay focussed on getting them done one step at a time. Where Focus Goes, Energy Flows!

The end.

On: Forgiving

Once upon a time, there were two friends named Jack and Sarah. They were the best of friends and did everything together.

One day they had a disagreement, and while they both still tried to be kind to each other, neither one wanted to forgive the other. Jack felt his pride had been hurt, so he didn't want to accept an apology, while Sarah was so hurt that she refused to acknowledge any wrongdoing on her part.

The days went by, but the tension between them continued. Sarah finally worked up the courage to talk it out with Jack. She said, "Jack, I know we have been in a bad place recently, but if we don't learn how to forgive then our friendship will never get back on track." Jack knew she was right, but he was still hesitant as he hadn't forgotten how much he had been hurt by their disagreement.

Sarah then asked him gently, "What would you do if I had done something wrong? Would you not want to forgive me?" That's when it hit him: nobody is perfect, and everyone makes mistakes. yet if we want others to forgive us for our mistakes. then we must learn how to forgive those who have wronged us too.

Jack took a deep breath and told Sarah that he could work on forgiving her. Even though it wasn't easy for either of them. he explained that this would require each of them to understand what happened from the other's point of view and accepting responsibility for their part in the disagreement. no matter how small that part may have been.

Sarah nodded in agreement and thanked Jack for his willingness to forgive her. despite being hurt by the situation herself. From that moment forward. they worked hard at communicating more honestly with each other and practiced forgiving freely whenever things got tough between them. In the end. their friendship flourished more than ever before.

This story teaches us an important lesson: even when things get tough between people who care about each other deeply. it is always important to practice forgiveness as it can help make relationships stronger than ever before.

The end.

On: Friendship

Once upon a time there was a little girl called Amy. She was starting her first day of school and she was feeling nervous. She wanted to make lots of new friends. but she didn't know who to choose.

That's when Amy heard an old saying: "Show me your friends and I'll show you who you are." What did it mean?

Amy decided to take the saying to heart. so she started by looking around for people who shared her interests. Through trial and error. she eventually found some great friends who liked the same things she did — books. art. and music. Being with these new friends made her feel confident and happy in school.

They were all kind-hearted too. which was something else Amy valued in a friend. She noticed that being around them meant that she became more considerate in return. They encouraged her to be the best version of herself. rather than holding her back or dragging her down.

Amy also learned about the advantages of having good friends at school. Not only could they provide emotional support on a tough day, they could help each other out with work or projects too. Their friendship grew stronger over time and soon Amy felt like part of a family at school.

But, just as there are advantages to having good friends, there are disadvantages to associating with the wrong group of people at school. Having bad friends could lead to getting into trouble. It might even lead to committing crimes without realising it because it's all too easy to be led astray by peers.

Just as it's important to have good friends, it's important to *be* a good friend too. Always remember that a friend in need is a friend indeed.

So, as long as you remember to surround yourself with positive influences, you can use the old "show me your friends and I'll show you who you are" saying as an effective tool to help shape your character from a young age.

The end.

On: Generosity

Once upon a time in a small village lived a young boy by the name of Jack. He was not very well off and had to live with his family in a small house. His parents never had enough money and Jack was always worried about them. He wanted to help but didn't know how.

One day he overheard two older men talking about how people were selfish and only thought of themselves. They said that if people were more generous. the world would be a better place. This struck a chord with Jack. and he decided that he must do something to make his community better.

The next day. Jack went around helping his neighbours wherever he could — carrying heavy buckets of water. picking up fallen branches after the storm. or playing with children so their parents could take breaks from their chores. By doing these simple tasks. Jack showed everyone what it means to give without expecting anything in return. His neighbours were touched by his kindness and generosity.

and soon word spread throughout the village about his good deeds.

As time passed by, more and more people started noticing Jack's kind nature and began offering him help whenever they could. His family's economic conditions slowly improved as they received food packages from their neighbours whose children they took care of while they worked.

Jack also helped many small businesses grow in the village. He shared his goods with everyone for free or at a discounted rate even when his own family was going through tough times financially. People not only appreciated this generous gesture but also made sure to buy those products from him once they could afford to.

Jack learnt an important lesson in life: sharing is indeed caring! Generosity towards others doesn't mean sacrificing your own needs, but rather understanding that we are all part of one big community where mutual respect and compassion can go a long way towards making everyone's lives better.

The end.

On: Good Habits

Once upon a time there was a little girl named Anna who often found herself getting into trouble. She would forget to do her homework, arrive late to parties, and even have occasional outbursts of anger when things didn't go her way. Her parents were starting to get worried about how this could affect her future if she didn't make some changes.

One day, Anna's mother had a chat with her about habits — good ones and bad ones. She explained that although it can be difficult, it is important to create good habits and to let go of the bad ones. Good habits are behaviours that bring us closer to where we want to be. For example, brushing your teeth every morning, or going for a run after school. Bad habits on the other hand, such as eating unhealthy snacks or staying up too late at night, can make it difficult for us to reach our goals and be our best selves.

Anna understood what her mother was saying but wondered how she could ever break free from all the bad habits she had acquired over the years. Her mum suggested starting small by setting small, attainable goals each day. An example could be taking 15 minutes each day to read something inspiring or learn something new instead of spending that time sitting around watching television.

The next step would be creating simple rewards in order to motivate yourself further. An example could be treating yourself with a small ice cream once you finish writing that essay you've been putting off for weeks!

Finally, don't forget about reflection. Spend some time each week thinking about whether or not you managed your goals well, and what areas you need to improve on so that you can start again fresh next week. Doing so will help you stay motivated and encourage further success as you build more good habits over time.

Anna soon realised that living by these principles was far from easy but, with determination and dedication she slowly became more aware of which habits were helpful in her life and which were holding her back. Once she recognised the difference, she began letting go of the unhelpful ones and making sure only the good habits remained.

The end.

On: Gratitude

Once upon a time there was a little girl who always felt like she did not have enough. Despite having all that she needed, she often complained and focused on what she lacked.

One day her grandmother visited and told her the importance of being grateful for all the wonderful things in life. Gratitude, she explained, is the appreciation of what one already has instead of focusing on what one does not have. She encouraged the little girl to take a look around her and be thankful for all the blessings that were present in her life.

The little girl followed her grandmother's advice and began expressing gratitude every single day. Whenever something good happened to her, or she received an unexpected blessing, she counted it as an opportunity to be thankful for whatever situation she was in. She soon found herself feeling happier and more content with life, despite any hardships or obstacles that might come up.

Every day, the little girl thanked God for all the wonderful gifts He gave her and asked Him for help during difficult times. Even when things didn't go as planned, she always made sure to express gratitude for where she was right then and there, which helped make those hard times easier to bear.

The little girl's story is proof that gratitude can truly bring happiness in any situation — whether it's good or bad — because it helps us become aware of our blessings. It also brings with it the privilege of contentment no matter where we are in life's journey. Gratitude allows us to appreciate small moments of joy as well as difficult lessons learned along the way. It helps us become successful by reminding us just how blessed we are, even during challenging circumstances.

The end.

On: Humility

Once upon a time in a far-off land, there lived a young prince who was known for his immense wealth and power. He had everything he could ever want or need, but he was not content with his life. He often felt lonely and empty despite all his material possessions.

One day, the prince decided to go on a journey. Along the way he encountered many people of different backgrounds and experiences, and these people opened up his eyes to a different kind of world — one that focused less on material possessions and more on empathy and humility.

At first, the prince was unsure why everyone seemed so content with their lives when they had so little compared to him. But then he found himself wondering how different his life would be if he embraced the same values as these humble people did.

He slowly began to understand the concept of humbleness. It is letting go of ego-driven desires like comparing oneself with others, trying to gain power over those around you, or pursuing selfish interests without considering their effects on others. Humility is an attitude that puts other people's needs before our own: it encourages us to be grateful for what we have rather than endlessly striving for more: it helps us develop meaningful relationships by sharing our successes and failures honestly: it allows us to be vulnerable enough to ask for help when needed: and it teaches us to stay grounded even when success arrives at our doorstep.

The prince realised that although humility may not bring about immediate rewards like notoriety or wealth, in the long run its benefits are invaluable, both personally and professionally. So, he decided to step back from his old ways of living and start living life with humility as its foundation. Only then would he be able to find true happiness within himself. The prince also thought about how being humble can influence those around us too. If we aim to set an example by showing attention and care towards others while staying away from any actions motivated solely by ego, then those around us will surely strive towards greater heights themselves.

Finally, the prince returned home. He had changed in many ways, and was now filled with gratitude for all that life had blessed him with despite his earlier misgivings. He was determined never to forget what he had learned from humbleness during his travels. He knew that though it may not always lead you directly down the path of fame or fortune, its value can never be underestimated.

And so ends this story featuring our wise young prince who understood that though being powerful is undoubtedly attractive in today's world, being humble will get you much further!

The end.

On: Integrity

Once upon a time, there was a little boy named Ian who lived in a small village. He was always recognised by the villagers for his honesty and fairness.

His parents had instilled in him the importance of integrity since he was young. Integrity is all about having moral strength to stay true to yourself and your beliefs, no matter what. It means doing the right thing, even when it's difficult or unpopular.

Integrity is about being honest and truthful in all things, and treating others with respect even if you don't agree with them. Ian knew that having personal integrity meant that people trusted him, respected him, and valued his word.

So, whenever someone asked Ian for help or advice, they knew they could count on him to tell them the truth no matter what. The advantages of being known as a person of integrity are numerous. People want you to sit on their team because they know you can be trusted; your friends value your opinion because they know that it is honest; people offer you jobs because they trust that you will do the job properly and not take shortcuts; employers give you promotions because they appreciate your loyalty; and those closest to you rely on your reliability and dependability in times of need.

On the other hand, not having personal integrity has its consequences. People may think twice before asking for help; friends may start avoiding conversations about important topics because they don't trust what you say; employers won't give you trustworthy assignments; and worst of all, those close to you may begin to doubt whether or not they can really depend on you.

The good news is that developing personal integrity isn't hard. It's something anyone can learn with practice. Here are five ways to start building more integrity into your life:

1. Speak your truth without fear — When faced with making a tough decision, stand up for what's right, instead of going along with everyone else out of fear of repercussions or rejection.

2. Respect other people's opinions — Don't belittle others' views or discount their feelings just because they're different from yours. Instead, try to understand where they're coming from, even if it doesn't align with what you believe or feel.

3. Follow through on commitments — Do what you say when promised — no excuses! Not only does this build trust around others, it will also make sure that important tasks get done properly and on time each time without fail.

4. Apologise when wrong — Nobody's perfect. We all make mistakes at some point in our lives! Showing humility when wrong and taking responsibility shows maturity as well as personal growth, which helps foster relationships built on mutual respect rather than suspicion or judgemental behaviour.

5. Be open minded — Keeping an open mind can help prevent our own biases from clouding our judgement when considering new ideas or points-of-view offered by others that may differ greatly from ours. This allows us to evaluate situations

objectively while staying honest and true to ourselves at all times.

Ian learned these lessons early in life and soon grew into a man respected throughout the entire village. All because his character was framed by one unwavering virtue: integrity!

The end.

On: Kindness

Once upon a time there was a village called Kindness.
It was filled with people who were kind to one another and
helped each other in any way they could.

The villagers of Kindness valued kindness above all else.
They believed that being kind to others was the most
important thing you could do in life and that it made them
better people.

Every morning, the villagers of Kindness would start their
day with a simple but powerful reflection: "What can I do
today to show kindness?"

Each day brought new opportunities to help somebody else
or make someone else feel better. The villagers knew that by
showing kindness, they were making a positive difference in
the world — something that couldn't be measured in money
or status.

The importance of kindness was taught to the children
from an early age. They learned about the benefits of being

kind, such as feeling good about helping others and making friends easier. As they grew older, they understood its importance even more, seeing how it could make difficult situations easier or solve disagreements between family members and friends.

Being kind is also beneficial for your own peace of mind. When you act kindly towards others, it helps you think positively about yourself and increases your self-esteem. As an additional bonus, when you are known for being kind, people are more likely to approach you and enjoy spending time with you.

However, not everybody in the village saw kindness as a virtue. Some saw it as a weakness. For example, if someone did something wrong, they thought they could just get away with it because others wouldn't punish them due to their kind nature. Unfortunately, this attitude shows that these people don't understand the true power of kindness — which is only realised when given selflessly without expecting anything in return.

No matter what opinion anyone holds on kindness, Kindness Village will continue as it is forever.

It will continue to teach others around them what
really matters, and that is that acting as though
we are all connected through our common humanity is
essential for creating a better world for everyone
to live in.

The end.

On: Leadership

Once upon a time there was a young boy who wanted to show leadership. He had heard many stories about great leaders that could inspire people, and thought he could do the same.

So, he set out to learn how to be a leader. He began reading books about leadership and talking to other kids his age who were also showing leadership in their own ways.

He quickly realised that being a leader was not about grandiosity or power but rather it was about understanding the needs of others, listening to their perspectives and providing support when needed. He understood that good leaders take initiative and are willing to help others in any way possible.

He also learned how important it is for leaders to be organised, responsible, honest, and open-minded; traits that would help him to become successful in the future.

The young boy started growing into an exemplary leader by setting examples for his friends and helping them solve problems they faced. He even began taking on more responsibility at home without being asked by his parents!

With practice, patience, and determination, the young boy started becoming a very capable leader and found himself surrounded by an inspiring community of supporters who believed in his abilities and valued his contributions.

The young boy's growth as a leader taught him valuable life lessons such as empathy, resilience, respect for authority figures, collaboration skills, crisis management techniques and problem-solving strategies, all of which he would need later on in life when facing bigger challenges at work or during university studies.

By developing these leadership habits early on in life, the young boy built up the confidence needed to tackle any obstacle — no matter how difficult it may seem.

The end.

On: Learning

Once upon a time there was a young girl named Ana. Ana loved to learn. and her parents saw how much she enjoyed it.

She would ask all kinds of questions about the world and took great delight in learning the answers. Her parents wanted her to know that learning is important. so they encouraged her to do her best in school and to make sure she was doing her homework.

Ana quickly realised that learning made life more enjoyable. as she discovered new things every day. She found that she could understand more complex concepts if she studied them closely. She also understood that by learning different skills. like playing an instrument or speaking a foreign language. it opened up new doors of opportunity for her future.

Ana soon began to see learning as a privilege and something she should take seriously. She understood that the more effort she put into her studies today. the better prepared she would be for tomorrow's challenges.

At school, Ana became one of the top students and always did well on tests and projects. She made many friends who admired how smart and hardworking she was. Everyone noticed how focused she was on staying ahead of the class so that when classes got tougher in high school, she already had a head start on the material.

When it came time for college applications, Ana's hard work paid off with acceptance letters from some of the best universities around the country. Even then, Ana continued to enjoy learning because she found it fascinating and rewarding — not just for career success but also as part of living a fulfilling life.

Throughout our lives we are constantly presented with opportunities to learn new things. It is our choice whether or not we take advantage of these chances. As Ana showed us all, having a passion for knowledge will always open up doors of opportunity, both now and in our future!

The end.

On: Listening

Once upon a time there was a little girl named Sarah. She lived with her parents in a cosy house filled with love and joy.

Sarah loved her parents very much and she knew that they only wanted what was best for her. Yet, there were times when Sarah would not listen to her parents. She would get angry and frustrated when she didn't get her way or even when being asked to help out around the house.

One day, Sarah's mother sat down with her to explain the importance of listening to your parents. "My darling," she said, "your father and I only want what is good for you, no matter how difficult it may seem. We understand that mistakes are part of growing up, but we can help you avoid some of them by sharing our experiences with you."

Sarah listened intently as her mother continued. "Sweetheart, it is important to remember that listening to our advice now will help you make fewer mistakes when you're older and managing life on your own. Furthermore, fostering a habit of listening to us will create harmony in our household so we won't be constantly arguing over every issue."

Little Sarah took this knowledge deep into her heart and from that day forward always tried her best to obey her loving parents' wishes. As she grew older, it became easier for Sarah to realise the advantages of listening to the advice of those who know what is best for us — especially our parents.

Listening became second nature for Sarah as she mastered the art of discernment between what was worth considering from others versus that which did not serve any purpose — especially coming from someone whose intentions were not pure or honest. In school, at work, and home alike, Sarah found success through applying the insights shared by her loving parents, and she avoided making the same mistakes they had made when they were young.

It wasn't always easy understanding why certain things needed to be done, but thanks to the trust developed between parent and child over many years, Sarah could look back fondly on those childhood days where learning such an important lesson ultimately shaped who she had become.

Over time, one thing above all else mattered: listening closely brought true happiness into their lives and created harmony in the household because more listening led to less fighting among family members!

The end.

On: Manners

Once upon a time there was a young boy called Tom. Tom was known for his good manners and polite demeanor. He always held doors open for others, said please and thank you, and treated all those around him with respect.

Tom's parents were very proud of his behaviour and often praised him for it. His friends were also impressed with how well-mannered he was, although sometimes they made fun of him behind his back.

One day, Tom's parents took him to a fancy restaurant for dinner. Tom remembered all his good manners: he walked in quietly and spoke softly, sat up straight and asked politely if someone needed something before helping himself. Everyone at the table noticed how well behaved he was. Even the waiter remarked on it.

The advantages of having good manners soon became clear to Tom. Everywhere he went people seemed to notice his politeness and kindness, which in turn encouraged those around him to be more courteous as well. He realised that by being respectful of others he gained their respect in return, which had helped him make friends at school and allowed him to get ahead in life.

Having good manners isn't just about proper etiquette in public, it also means being mindful of other people's feelings in any situation. This could be as simple as not speaking too loudly on the bus or train, or not drawing attention to yourself when you are out with your peers. Such small gestures can be just as important as remembering your table manners when eating out.

Having good manners helps build a positive reputation with others, which can lead to success later in life. Employers might look for candidates who have shown themselves to be polite and capable of dealing well with other people. Likewise, teachers may find students who show good conduct more pleasant to work with than those who do not display such behaviour.

All these factors point towards the importance of having good manners. They allow you to gain trust from those around you while also making yourself feel better by treating everyone kindly, even though you expect nothing in return.

So, always remember this: if you want to be successful both now and in the future, keep practicing your best behaviour whenever possible.

The end.

On: Moral Values

Once upon a time there was a group of children who wanted to learn about moral values. They asked their parents and teachers what it meant to have high moral values, and everyone had a different definition for them.

Moral values can be defined as the principles that guide the way someone should live their life ethically and responsibly. Examples of moral values include honesty, integrity, respect, kindness, fairness, and compassion.

The children learned that the advantages of having high moral values are numerous. It builds trust with others, allows them to make informed decisions using their conscience as guidance, and helps people build strong relationships based on mutual respect and understanding.

On the other hand, not having high moral values can lead to poor decision making because there's no ethical framework to provide a guide through life. People without morality may find themselves in difficult situations because they lack respect for those around them or use lies to get ahead.

The children also realised that developing these qualities from childhood could pay off in later life by helping them succeed at work or in personal relationships. Having strong morals will allow them to stay true to themselves and handle tough situations ethically instead of taking shortcuts or resorting to dishonesty.

In conclusion, the children learned that high moral values are essential for living a meaningful life full of positive relationships and success both professionally and personally. With these lessons in mind, they all promised each other that they would always strive to live with integrity, no matter what came their way.

The end.

On: Morning Routines

Once upon a time there lived a young girl named Claire. Claire was an ambitious and energetic student who loved nothing more than going to school each day.

Unfortunately, she was often overwhelmed by her morning routine, which usually left her feeling rushed and exhausted before the day had even begun.

One day, while daydreaming in school, she remembered something her mother had once told her: the best way to have a good day is to start your morning right. She sat up and determined that she would try just that. She would create a good morning ritual for herself.

The next day, Claire woke up thirty minutes earlier than usual and immediately opened up a book of stories. It was always important to read something positive first thing in the morning. After reading for ten minutes or so, she got out of bed and did some light stretches and exercises, knowing that exercise not only kickstarted her energy but also made her happier overall. Finally, after brushing her teeth and getting dressed for school, Claire took the time to make sure she had eaten a good breakfast. Her parents had taught her this was essential for staying sharp during classes.

Finishing all these steps with time to spare before school proved to be such a relief. Just as creating structure in your life helps you stay organised outside of school hours, starting your mornings off in a positive way ensures that you are prepared mentally and physically for whatever the day may bring.

Claire continued with this ritual every morning until it became second nature — almost like an automatic reflex each time she woke up. She found that reaching school on time each morning with energy levels still high made such a difference in her academic performance. Months later, when report cards came out, she had been awarded top marks due to being better prepared and attentive throughout classes. On top of that, following this routine also improved Claire's mood immensely, with most days starting off on an upbeat and optimistic note!

She realised that having a routine could be beneficial, no matter how big or small. If followed correctly, it could truly help set you up for success, no matter what task lay ahead.

The end.

On: Patience

Once upon a time there was a young boy named Timmy.

He was eager to try all new things and was always in a rush. He had a difficult time understanding what it meant to have patience.

One day, Timmy's mum took him to the park for some quality time together. Timmy saw an ice cream stand nearby and wanted to get one immediately. His mum told him that he would have to wait until the end of their outing at the park before they could stop for ice cream.

This made Timmy very frustrated as he had no concept of patience.

What is patience, one might ask? Patience is defined as having the ability to accept or tolerate delay, without becoming annoyed or anxious. It helps us stay calm and focused when faced with difficult situations or obstacles. Being patient allows us to think through our options and make better decisions, rather than just reacting impulsively in the moment.

The benefits of possessing patience are numerous. It helps foster healthy relationships with other people as well as ourselves, prevents unnecessary stress and frustration, and encourages understanding and open-mindedness towards others' perspectives and feelings, and so many other benefits.

Some examples of being patient are being able to stay calm while waiting in long lines at the grocery store, or being able to listen carefully without interrupting someone else when they are speaking.

On the other hand, not having patience can lead to negative outcomes like blaming others for our own mistakes or failures instead of taking responsibility, making rash decisions which may not be beneficial further down the line, and increased levels of anger and frustration due to unmet expectations. All this can significantly dampen our overall enjoyment in life if unchecked over time.

At the end of their trip to the park, Timmy's mum reminded him about his need for patience once again before finally getting him his much-desired ice cream treat.

From then on. Timmy started cultivating more tolerance towards situations that required him to be patient. Timmy eventually learned how blessed one can feel when they start living life with more mindfulness. thanks largely in part to having patience!

The end.

On: Peer Pressure

Once upon a time there was a little girl named Lily who lived in a small village. The villagers were all very kind and friendly, but they didn't always agree on the same things.

Every day after school, Lily and her friends would hang around and talk about their day. One day, one of her friends said that the cool kids were doing something exciting, like going to the river for swimming. But no one knew if it was allowed or not.

Everyone went along with what their friend said, because they wanted to fit in and be part of the group. Lily felt peer pressure pushing her to do what everyone else was doing. She really wanted to go along with them, even though she had a feeling that it wasn't a good idea.

She felt scared and confused by the thought of saying no to her friends, but Lily decided to stand up against the peer pressure. Even though she was scared, she voiced her opinion firmly and said, "No, I don't think this is the right thing to do." Everyone else got mad at her for being different. but Lily stuck with her decision despite it feeling hard for her.

It turned out that swimming in the river was actually very dangerous. If Lily had gone along with her friends instead of standing up against peer pressure, she could have been hurt. or worse. This is why it's so important to stand up against peer pressure, even when you're scared.

Doing so can save your life or keep you from getting into big trouble! Standing up against peer pressure shows strength and courage — two qualities every child should strive for. Not only does standing up against peer pressure keep you safe from danger, it has other advantages. It will make people respect you more when you take charge and make your own decisions rather than giving into what everyone else wants you to do.

And. most importantly, it will help build your self-esteem knowing that you made the right choice in an uncomfortable situation.

The end.

On: Perseverance

Once upon a time there lived a boy named John who had a passion for learning.

John was determined to succeed no matter what obstacles came his way. He was willing to put in the hard work and effort required to achieve his goals. This determination was his perseverance.

Perseverance is the quality of being determined to continue and keep going despite any challenges or difficulties that may arise. It allows one to remain focused on long-term goals instead of giving up when faced with short-term challenges or failures.

The benefits and advantages of having perseverance are numerous. Perseverance allows for better problem-solving skills as well as helping one gain confidence in their own abilities to overcome difficult situations or tasks. With this quality, people can develop better tenacity, patience, and resilience which are all important skills needed for life. Additionally, it can lead to greater accomplishments over time by providing motivation and drive to reach desired outcomes even during difficult times.

One example of how perseverance can pay off is when studying for an exam. Studying consistently over a period of time instead of cramming right before an exam could help increase comprehension and overall performance leading to better grades in the end.

On the other hand, not having perseverance can have some negative consequences. For instance, without perseverance, one may give up early on more daunting tasks without giving success a chance. This would lead to a lack of satisfaction with any accomplishments that had been achieved along the way, or could have been if given enough time.

Additionally, lacking this trait could prevent someone from reaching their full potential. Not pushing through difficult times that may otherwise have been conquered with enough persistence and dedication can only hold them back.

John was aware of these benefits, so he worked hard day after day until he eventually reached his goals, often much

quicker than others expected him too. His determination
paid off.

And with that, we see how having perseverance can be
beneficial in many ways. Even if you stumble along your
journey, there's nothing wrong with picking yourself back
up again and staying determined. Always remember that
hard work will pay off!

The end.

On: Positive Affirmations

Once upon a time there was a little girl named Maria.
She had the habit of speaking negatively to herself
when she did something wrong or messed up on a
homework assignment. Maria's mum noticed this and
wanted to help her daughter become more confident
and happy in life, so she introduced her to positive
affirmations.

Positive affirmations are phrases that you repeat over
and over again in your head. Things like "I am strong"
or "I am smart" that will help to build confidence and
self-esteem.

Every morning before school, Maria's mum would tell her
five different positive affirmations to say in her head
throughout the day. Some of those included:

1. "I can do anything I set my mind to."
2. "My dreams are within reach."
3. "I will stay focused and face any challenge that comes
   my way with courage."

4. "Today is going to be a great day!"
5. "I have everything I need to succeed."

Maria soon realised the power of these positive affirmations. It put her in a better state of mind each time she repeated them, helping her stay motivated throughout the school day and beyond. Whenever she felt overwhelmed by an assignment or test, she thought back to these words for encouragement and support.

Before long, Maria was seeing results from all her hard work. She began receiving compliments from her teachers about how well she was doing in school and started feeling more confident about herself overall as she continued saying these positive affirmations each morning before classes started. She even shared them with some of her classmates who also found them helpful for keeping themselves encouraged during their studies too.

Maria was very thankful for how much confidence the positive affirmations brought her. They gave her the strength to make it through tough times at school, as well as making studying feel less intimidating overall.

Without those powerful words, Maria would not have seen nearly as much success as she had in the classroom and in her life. They helped instil faith and perseverance into her everyday routine, and this ultimately allowed her to achieve greatness!

The end.

On: Positive Energy

Once upon a time there was a little girl named Mia who loved to smile and spread positivity to everyone around her. Everywhere she went, she left behind a sprinkle of joy that made all the people around her feel happy and good about themselves.

Mia knew it was important to be kind and selfless in every situation. She understood that if you have positive energy, you can add something special to any conversation. Whenever Mia had an opportunity, she didn't think twice about doing something nice for someone else, regardless of what she got back in return.

One day, while walking down the street, Mia noticed a woman sitting on the ground with her head bowed low. It seemed that the woman was having a really bad day, so Mia decided to do something special for her. She walked over and asked if there was anything she could do to help brighten up her day. After talking it through with Mia, the woman's attitude changed completely. She felt so much better after that conversation!

Mia learned that day that having positive energy is contagious. When you give off good vibes or show kindness to others, they will often reciprocate your kindness and spread it further around them. Being selfless can be difficult but it makes a massive difference in how other people perceive us and increases our own personal happiness too!

This experience taught Mia an important lesson: never underestimate the power of giving off positive energy instead of negative energy, no matter what situation you're in. From then on, Mia always strived to keep her energy levels high wherever she went so that everybody around her benefited from its effects.

The end.

On: Positive Language

Once upon a time there lived a young boy named Jimmy. His parents always taught him to be kind and use polite language when talking.

Sadly, Jimmy had difficulty remembering this valuable lesson. Whenever he encountered something challenging or difficult, his first reaction was to say something negative rather than positive.

One day, his parents decided it was time for him to learn the power of using positive words when communicating. They told him a story about their own experiences with negative words. They explained how hurtful certain words can be, both to others and to himself, and especially those self-defeating comments he often used in times of stress or difficulty.

Then they asked him to think of another way to express himself without being so harsh. They reminded him that speaking positively is not only beneficial for those around him but also for himself. Positive speech reflects on one's character in a very good way and opens up doors for better relationships, opportunities, and overall wellbeing.

Jimmy began to pay attention to what came out of his mouth. From then on, he started practicing using uplifting words when talking to himself and others. He found that changing his language gave him the courage and strength needed to face any challenge head-on.

Instead of claiming, "This homework is impossible," he would try, "Let me break it down step by step until I understand it clearly." Instead of responding with, "It will never work out!" he would choose to believe, "I'm sure I'll find the right way soon enough."

Jimmy soon realised how powerful it could be when one chooses the right words in any given situation. No matter how hard it seemed at first, these encouraging expressions kept lifting his spirit up higher every single time.

And before long, Jimmy learned just how much of an effect proper communication could have on himself as well as those around him. His positive language brought joy into everyone's life at home!

The end.

On: Positive Thinking

Once upon a time there was a young boy named Colin who often felt overwhelmed by the world. He had been told that he needed to be more positive. but didn't really know what this entailed. One day. while walking through the forest. he stumbled across a wise old lady holding a magical crystal ball. Colin asked the wise old lady what people meant by "positive thinking"? She told him that positive thinking was the magic power we all possess deep inside us. a power that lets us achieve whatever we put our minds to.

This fascinated Colin. and he asked her to explain further. The wise old lady explained that positive thinking is having an optimistic attitude and believing in yourself and your abilities. It's about focusing on possibilities rather than limits. It's also having self-confidence and looking for solutions instead of problems.

She went on to say that there are many benefits of positive thinking. It boosts happiness. lowers stress levels. increases concentration levels. helps with solving problems. improves relationships. and even helps with physical health.

Colin wished that he could change his negative thoughts into positive ones and asked the wise old lady for help. "How can I turn my negative thinking into positive thinking?" he asked. The wise old lady gave him some good advice. She said he should practice affirmations such as "I'm capable" or "I will succeed." and to think about all the things he was thankful for. She told him to focus on the positives in any situation. instead of dwelling on the negatives. and to always remember that failure is just another way of learning how to do something better next time.

Back at school. Colin found that positive thinking had many advantages. It improved his grades because he was more focused on his studies. he made more friends as people were attracted to his upbeat outlook on life, and he developed stronger relationships with teachers due to their mutual trust.

Later on in life. Colin often thought back on the encounter with the wise old lady he stumbled across while walking through the forest. and how that encounter and lessons learned helped create a brighter future for him. Since that day. nothing had seemed impossible for Colin.

The end.

On: Procrastinating

Once upon a time there was a young girl named
Lucy. Lucy was always looking forward to fun activities.
like visiting the park and playing with her friends.
But when it came to doing simple tasks like cleaning
her room or doing her homework. she just couldn't do
it. She'd tell herself that she'd do it later. but before
she knew it. later had already come and gone! Lucy was
procrastinating.

But what is procrastinating? Procrastination is when
you keep putting off something that needs to be done.
It can be anything. such as cleaning your room to doing
your homework. and it usually happens when the task feels
overwhelming or boring.

When we procrastinate. we put off taking action
and this can have a negative impact on us. It can
mean missing deadlines or opportunities. feeling
stressed and overwhelmed. or not having enough time
for important things. And this is exactly what happened
to Lucy.

Lucy began missing deadlines for school assignments and losing out on opportunities to play with her friends. What's even worse, it never felt good knowing that she had put something off until the last minute; the feeling of stress would overwhelm her every time.

It didn't take long for Lucy to realise that procrastination wasn't doing her any favours. So one day, when faced with another task that she wanted to delay, she decided enough was enough.

Instead of putting off what needed to be done until tomorrow, Lucy gave herself small goals throughout the day. These were tasks such as finishing a chapter in her book before lunchtime, or tidying up her bedroom by dinner time.

Setting these specific goals made it much easier for her to accomplish them. Once Lucy got into an orderly routine where everything was taken care of on time, she found so many other benefits. Her grades improved as she no longer risked forgetting an assignment or submitting it late. And best of all, Lucy never felt stressed again once things were kept up-to-date and organised.

So remember. don't wait around too long when you have something important you need to do. Set yourself some manageable goals and stay on top of your responsibilities. That way. you won't ever miss out on the good things life has in store for you!

The end.

On: Reflection

Once upon a time there was a young student named Tom. Tom was always looking for ways to grow and become a better person. One day, his teacher introduced him to a concept called reflection.

Tom asked his teacher what it meant to reflect on something that happened. His teacher explained that it meant taking the time to think deeply and analyse an experience or event, and to understand how the things in your life affect you personally. Additionally, reflecting on one's past can be incredibly helpful in making decisions for the future.

Tom's teacher instructed him to make a habit of reflecting for 10 minutes at the end of each day. This meant writing down his thoughts about what went well that day and thinking of positive steps he could have taken to remedy any negative experiences or things that didn't go so well that day. Tom thought this would be difficult at first, but he was determined to try it out.

At first. he found the practice overwhelming. Trying to figure out exactly what went well and not so well during each day seemed daunting and tedious. But. over time. Tom found himself growing more comfortable with reflecting on his days and viewing them from different perspectives.

When he felt down about certain events. Tom realised he could take another look at them with a different attitude. This made it easier for him to identify potential solutions he wouldn't have seen before without analysing things further.

Before long. reflection had become an integral part of Tom's daily routine. Even when things were going great at school. he still took some time at night just to review how his day went and to think of ways that tomorrow could be even better!

Tom was amazed by the power of reflection and how much good it had brought into his life. He now felt equipped with the skills necessary to approach challenges head-on. His teacher was proud too. It was clear that all her guidance had paid off tenfold.

The end.

On: Reputation

Once upon a time there was a young girl named Lily. Lily knew that the reputation she had with her peers was important. so she worked hard to maintain a good image and be seen positively by those around her.

Lily's parents taught her early on that having a good reputation is essential. because it's the most valuable asset one can possess in life. A good reputation opens doors. brings trust and respect. and gives you credibility in any situation. So Lily tried to keep up with this advice whenever possible.

At school. Lily found out pretty quickly that having a good reputation brought many benefits. She made friends easily and people listened to her when she spoke up in class. If she needed help from teachers or other students. they were all willing to lend her a hand. knowing her for who she really was and trusting her word.

But what exactly builds a good reputation? In general. it's simple things like being kind to others. doing the right thing even when no one is watching, showing respect towards authority figures and elders, and making smart decisions based on facts rather than feelings or emotions. All these qualities build up gradually over time into a strong positive image of yourself in others' minds.

By comparison, bad behaviour such as lying or cheating will result in negative consequences that can hurt your reputation more than anything else — especially when someone finds out about them! Being unkind to others will also bring about a bad reputation because nobody likes people who are mean or rude for no reason at all.

In the end, Lily found out for herself how having a good reputation at school helped shape the person she became. She knows her reputation will stay with her throughout life, helping her to land her dream job, find true friendship, and so many other good things along the way. She understands that having a good name is an essential part of living a good life.

The end.

On: Respect

Once upon a time there were two friends named John and Jane. One day, they were playing in the park when they came across some people who were behaving badly.

John was taken aback by their behaviour and said to Jane. "That's not how we should behave! We need to show respect to each other."

Jane agreed but asked John what he meant by respect. John thought for a moment before replying. "Respect is about giving people the same courtesy you would want for yourself. It's about listening to what others have to say and being polite in response."

John showed an example of respect when he offered his seat on the bus to an elderly person who looked tired. He didn't expect anything in return. but it made him feel good inside.

Jane also showed an example of respect when she used gentle words to speak to her younger siblings. even when she was feeling frustrated or angry. She knew it was always important to show kindness, even in hard situations, because it helps build strong relationships.

When they arrived home, John and Jane tried to think of more ways they could demonstrate respect to those around them. They decided that being supportive of everyone's individual differences would be a great way of showing respect for others, whether it was differences in someone's skin colour, beliefs, or opinions, they knew everyone should be free to express themselves without fear of judgement from others.

John and Jane understood that no matter how small or insignificant something may seem, if we demonstrate respect towards one another then we will create a kinder world together. As the poet Kahlil Gibran once said: "Treat everyone with politeness, even those who are rude to you — not because they are nice, but because you are!" This inspiring quote reminded them that self-respect is key. If you don't learn how to treat yourself right, then it won't be possible for you practice true respect towards others.

John and Jane both knew that mutual respect was essential if we all want to live peacefully together in harmony. Respect means understanding each other's differences, and allowing everyone equal opportunities regardless of any prejudices or personal biases that might otherwise exist between us all.

The end.

On: Responsibility

Once upon a time there was a young boy named Arthur who made some bad decisions. He had been warned by his parents that these actions would have consequences. but he chose to ignore their warnings.

One day. Arthur made yet another poor decision and found himself in a precarious situation. When he saw the situation he was in. he could have run away or tried to make excuses. however Arthur knew that if he wanted to learn from his mistakes then he must be accountable for what he had done.

So. despite the fear of punishment. Arthur stayed and faced the consequences of his actions bravely. To everybody's surprise. instead of punishing him. his parents praised him for taking responsibility for what he had done. They told him how proud they were of him for not running away and making excuses but rather facing the repercussions like an adult.

Arthur learned an important lesson about responsibility that day. It is better to be honest and face your mistakes than ignore them and try to forget about it all together. He learned that there are of course consequences to taking risks. but learning from our mistakes and being responsible can help us grow in life.

The next time Arthur was faced with a difficult task. or something he had done that he shouldn't have. he bravely faced the truth instead of running away or making excuses. He took ownership of his actions. no matter how tough it got. and this attitude earned him respect from his peers and family members alike.

In the end. by learning to take responsibility for his own actions. no matter how bad they might have been. Arthur learnt valuable lessons in life which helped him become wiser with every passing day!

The end.

On: Rest and Sleep

Once upon a time there was a boy called Jack. Jack was an eager and smart student who wanted to do his best in school, but time and time again he struggled to focus on his schoolwork.

Jack was used to staying up late, and then he struggled to get up in the morning in good time to prepare for going to school. As result, he often felt tired and sluggish at school, but he never thought much of it. Then, one day, Jack's teacher noticed that he seemed particularly distracted.

His teacher asked him if he was getting enough rest and sleep each night. Jack thought about it for a moment. He had been going to bed later and later each night as the days went by, making it hard for him to get up in the mornings.

His teacher then explained why getting enough rest is very important. When you get enough rest and sleep, your body can store energy so you can focus better during the day.

Jack realised that if he wanted to do well in school he'd have to make sure to get at least eight hours of sleep every night. That way, he could make sure his brain stayed focused throughout the day without feeling too sleepy or distracted.

Jack began implementing habits and routines that would make it easier for him to fall asleep earlier each night. He turned off all electronics an hour before bed time, read a book instead of scrolling through his phone, took a hot bath or shower before bedtime, and wrote down thoughts or worries before lying down in bed so they wouldn't keep him up all night long.

Having good sleeping habits allowed Jack to not only feel more energised during the day, it also gave him more mental clarity on tests and projects — something he hadn't expected.

Slowly but surely, Jack saw how beneficial getting enough rest and sleep each night was for both his physical health and his mental wellbeing. He lowered his stress levels and increased his ability to focus on any sort of activity or task that came along.

And so the lesson is clear. Getting enough rest isn't just important. it's essential!

Bedtime doesn't have to be boring either. With a few healthy habits like setting boundaries between school and playtime . creating a comfortable sleeping environment. eating healthy snacks. and exercising regularly. anyone can ensure they stay active and energized throughout their daily life.

The end.

On: Sadness

Once upon a time, there was a little girl named Lilly. Lilly was a very happy child and she felt like nothing could ever bring her down.

One day, something changed in Lilly's life, and she became really sad. She felt like no one understood her or even cared about how she felt.

Nothing seemed to make her happy anymore, not even what used to be her favourite things. She started avoiding all of her friends and family, feeling like nobody could possibly help her with what she was going through.

Lilly's parents noticed the change in their daughter and decided to talk to her about it. They asked Lilly why she had been feeling so sad lately, but they already knew the answer: sometimes life just brings sadness, no matter how hard we try to stay positive and happy.

They explained to their daughter that it's perfectly OK to feel sad every once in a while. It doesn't mean anything is wrong with us. it's just something that happens to everyone from time to time.

They then gave Lilly some advice on how to cope with those feelings of sadness. This was to talk about those feelings with someone she trusted (like her parents, teachers, or counsellors), to do activities that made her feel better (such as getting exercise, writing down her thoughts, or listening to music), to have patience (because things don't get solved overnight), to pray, and to try new things, perhaps even finding something she's good at and enjoys in the process.

They also explained the difference between sadness and depression. While both are perfectly natural reactions to experiences we have in life, depression, especially when it lasts for a long time, is something more serious that sometimes requires professional help.

After this conversation with her parents, Lilly started feeling much better. She still had moments when things were hard for her, and all those feelings of sadness came back, but she now knew these were normal emotions that everyone has, and she knew that talking about them would help.

She also realised that however bad things may seem. everything will be okay again. She knew this because she had people around her who cared about her. helping her to stay strong.

The end.

On: Self-Belief

Once upon a time, in a small town far away, there lived
a young girl named Julia. Julia was very determined and
goal-oriented, but she didn't have many friends because of
her shyness. She would often be discouraged by the people
around her who said that she couldn't achieve her dreams,
so she decided to prove them wrong.

Julia worked hard every day to achieve what she wanted in
life. Her hard work soon began to pay off, and people started
noticing her talent. However, despite her success, some
people still laughed at her and said that nothing she did
mattered. This was because it was only talent they saw, and
not the hard work behind it.

One day, while walking home from school, Julia found a
mysterious old man sitting on the curb. He looked at Julia with
a warm smile on his face and he asked her what was bothering
her. She told him about all the comments the other kids had
made and how discouraged she felt. The old man told Julia
not to worry about what other people say because believing in

yourself is more important than anything else. "You can be whatever you set your mind to." he said reassuringly. "No matter how talented someone might be. if they don't put in the effort then their talent won't get them far."

Julia nodded in agreement as an understanding grew within her. Believing in herself was key to achieving success no matter what anyone else said or thought about her abilities or talents. The old man stood up and gave Julia one final piece of advice: "Whatever your mind can conceive and believe. it can achieve."

From that moment on. Julia never forgot those words of wisdom. Whenever life threw obstacles into her path. she stopped for a moment to remember that believing in herself would always be key to achieving whatever she wanted. Just as the mysterious old man had told her. reaching her goals in life came down to believing that she could do it. No matter how big or small those goals were. commitment to reaching them was all that really mattered. No matter what others thought. Julia knew if she believed in herself. she could achieve everything she desired.

The end.

On: Selflessness

Once upon a time there was a small village on the outskirts of a bustling city. This village was home to many happy people who helped each other in times of need, and supported one another through thick and thin.

One day, a young boy named Jaden was walking through the village when he spotted an old man struggling to carry his heavy bags of wheat. Without any hesitation, Jaden quickly ran over to offer assistance.

He kindly offered to carry the old man's bags for him so he could walk more easily. The old man was overwhelmed by Jaden's kindness and selflessness. He thanked him profusely and explained that this kind act meant more to him than just being able to get home without being weighed down by his bags of grain. It meant that even at his age, someone still saw him as worthy of help and respect.

Jaden's story shows us what it means to be selfless. It is having consideration for others, and considering the needs of others before our own. It is focusing on bringing joy and happiness to others despite our own hardships or struggles. Selflessness can also mean providing support and comfort with no expectation of anything in return, or without expecting anything from anyone else apart from compassion for all living things.

The importance of being selfless cannot be overstated. By being kind and helpful towards others, without looking for anything in return, we are making the world a happier place — one person at a time! This also encourages others to do the same, which leads to more acts of kindness being spread around the world.

Practicing selflessness can start with small gestures such as holding doors open for people, or offering help when we see somebody struggling with something. Additionally, volunteering at shelters or donating funds are also great ways of displaying our care towards those around us.

No matter how small or big our actions might be, whenever we choose to show kindness and empathy towards people, it is an act of selflessness that goes a long way.

The lesson in the story is that there is a lot of joy in being selfless. This is the opposite of being selfish. Being selfish is focusing on yourself first, before considering anyone else's needs. Selfishness will ultimately lead to unhappiness, whereas being selfless makes the world a better place, one act at a time.

The end.

On: Self-Love

Once upon a time there was a little girl named Lucy who had always been taught to be kind and generous to others. But, what she didn't understand was that in order for her kindness to truly shine, she needed to start with herself first.

One day, as she was flying on an aeroplane with her family, the flight attendant announced that everyone should place their own oxygen mask on first before helping those around them. This got Lucy thinking — why put your own mask on before helping others?

The little girl soon realised it was because loving yourself and taking care of your own needs comes first. Only by loving and taking care of yourself can you be the best version of yourself for others. It's like spreading sunshine. When people are happy with themselves, they can spread even more happiness to those around them.

Lucy realised the importance of self-love and how it changed everything — both her relationships with herself and those around her. She focused on being kinder to herself by listening to her body and mind, taking time away from technology, practicing good sleep habits, eating healthy foods that help fuel her body, and most importantly, remembering that mistakes are part of learning.

With these new practices in place, Lucy saw a shift in how confident she felt within herself. This was something that radiated outwards into other areas of her life too, such as her performance in school, and in forming healthier relationships with others.

Lucy knew if everyone took the time to show more self-love, then the world would be a happier place for everyone. So, if there is one thing we can all learn from Lucy's story, it's this: self-love is essential, not just for ourselves, but also for the whole world around us.

The end.

On: Setting Goals

Once upon a time there was a young girl called Ava who dreamed of becoming an astronaut. She had big ambitions and wanted to be the best she could be. But, like many children, she often found herself feeling overwhelmed or lost on her journey.

One day, Ava's parents gave her some advice that would change her life forever: "Set Goals!"

Setting goals can help you become the best version of yourself.

But what do we mean by setting goals? Goals are like plans for the future that can help you learn and grow as a person. They can be short-term, like studying hard for a test tomorrow, or long-term, like becoming an astronaut when you grow up.

When you set goals for yourself, it gives you something to look forward to and strive for, which helps increase your motivation and give you a sense of accomplishment when you reach your goal.

Goal setting also helps us stay organised and productive because we can break down big tasks into smaller chunks, prioritise activities, and track our progress, allowing us to make changes if needed.

For performance-based activities like sports or music, setting goals is really important because it allows us to focus our efforts on achieving the end result. Doing this helps improve performance levels over time.

It also helps us understand ourselves better so we can discover our strengths and weaknesses.

Ava soon realised how important it was to set goals for herself so that she could reach her full potential in life!

The moral of this story is that everyone should strive for something greater than themselves by setting realistic yet meaningful goals — no matter how young or old we may be.

The end.

On: Standards

Once upon a time there was a young boy named Tommy who always struggled to remember to do his homework, his chores, and to live up to the moral standards that were expected of him.

But one day, his parents sat him down and reminded him of a motto: "How you do something is how you do everything." They explained the meaning of this motto to him by saying that if he would only make an effort to consistently do things to a high standard, rather than merely doing them when it suited him or seemed convenient, then he could build himself a good reputation.

Tommy took this lesson on board and slowly but surely he began to make an effort in all areas of his life. He asked for help when completing his revised homework and he made sure that the work was thoroughly completed rather than just finishing it off as fast as possible. When completing chores such as taking out the garbage, Tommy made sure that each task was done properly instead of cutting corners here and there.

Finally, when interacting with others, or making decisions about important matters, Tommy tried his best to consider the moral implications before making his choices, so that he could guarantee everything he did was done with high standards in mind.

As time passed by, people noticed how consistent Tommy had become. He was adhering to high standards across the board in all areas of life, no longer just in some areas. They respected him more for having such high expectations and admired how well rounded he had become, thanks to following the important motto shared by his parents.

And, while we may not always appreciate it at first, setting yourself goals and striving for higher standards within any area of your life can be extremely rewarding in many ways. Not just for what others may think, but for our own feeling of self-worth too. After all, "how you do something is how you do everything!"

The end.

On: Staying Healthy

Once upon a time there lived a young girl named Sally. Sally was an active and energetic child who spent her days playing in the park and running around with her friends. As Sally grew older, she began to realise that being healthy was more than just running around and playing games. It was about making good choices for her body and mind.

Sally wanted to make sure she could stay healthy and strong so she could continue doing all the things she loved. She learned that eating a balanced diet full of fresh fruits, vegetables, and whole grains was essential to help her grow big and strong, while also giving her enough energy to continue doing all of the things she enjoyed.

Sally also learned how important it was to get plenty of rest each day since it is during sleep that our bodies can heal and regenerate. This means we will be able to stay healthier and stronger if we get enough shut eye! Exercise was also incredibly important. Not only did it give her a great way to have fun, it helped keep her heart healthy too.

As Sally got older, she noticed how having healthy habits today would pay dividends tomorrow, and later in life. Not only would she feel better physically, but also mentally. She would find herself feeling calmer, more focused, and with more energy than ever before. Developing healthy habits from a young age helped her in school when studying for exams, in sport when preparing for competitions, and then those habits continued to pay off into adulthood.

Sally soon realised that the benefits of being healthy extend far beyond our physical self. By taking care of ourselves both inside and out, we can live a fuller life filled with joy and happiness. With this newfound wisdom, Sally set out on her journey towards becoming the healthiest version of herself possible, knowing that all the hard work would pay off in the end.

Not every journey is easy, but Sally's will always remind us of something very valuable: developing good habits while we are young is essential to living a healthier life now and into our future!

The end.

On: The Golden Rule

Once upon a time there was a little boy named Jack who, despite being very kind-hearted, often found himself struggling to get along with others. He would make jokes and tease his friends. He thought this was funny, but his jokes would often make them feel bad or hurt.

One day, one of Jack's friends came over and showed him something he had been learning in school. It was the "Golden Rule." This rule stated that if you want to be treated well, you should always treat others the same way. Jack was very intrigued by this and asked how he could put it into practice.

His friend explained that if you treat someone badly then they will probably treat you badly back — just like if you are kind to someone then they will most likely be nice to you in return. His friend went on to explain that no matter who it is, whether it's your family, your friends, or even strangers, everyone deserves respect and kindness for no reason other than it's just the right thing to do.

Jack thought about this for some time and decided that from now on he would try his best to live by the Golden Rule. He would do his best to handle situations in such a way that he treated everyone fairly, respectfully, and generously. He admitted that it wasn't always easy, but whenever he found himself in a difficult situation involving other people, he asked himself what the right thing to do would be according to the Golden Rule.

This helped him act in a better way towards others, whether it was helping friends with homework to improve their grades, or simply giving a friendly compliment when someone needed cheering up! Soon, those he interacted with began to feel more loved and accepted than ever before, all thanks to the respect and kindness he gave freely.

Jack also found he made many new friends by treating everyone with the same respect and kindness, and he gained new respect for himself too. He knew that regardless of any differences between people or any situation, everyone can benefit from living by the Golden Rule: always treat others as you would wish to be treated yourself.

The end.

On: The Law of Attraction

Once upon a time there lived a young girl named Emma. She was curious about the world and wanted to make her dreams come true.

One day, she heard about something called the Law of Attraction. She was intrigued by this idea and decided to learn as much as she could about it.

After some research, she learned that the Law of Attraction states that positive thoughts can attract positive outcomes, and negative thoughts can attract negative outcomes.

Emma began to experiment with the Law of Attraction on her own. She started by visualising and focusing on specific goals, such as doing well on a test or having an adventure with her friends.

Whenever something positive happened in her life, she attributed it to the power of her positive thoughts.

Emma also realised that she could use the Law of Attraction to work toward bigger goals, like getting into college or starting a business. To do this, Emma had to first set clear intentions for what she wanted to achieve, break down those goals into achievable steps, and focus on taking those steps every day. She found that if she kept up with this practice consistently, eventually she would find success in reaching her goals.

The impact of using the Law of Attraction for Emma was profound — it gave her control over her destiny! She found that good things kept coming her way because she was focused on creating them in her mind first.

However, Emma discovered that there were potential pitfalls when practicing the law of attraction. If she thought negatively, then more negative experiences would be attracted into her life instead. To avoid this, she had to ensure she kept an optimistic outlook while setting specific intentions, and kept taking consistent action towards them each day.

Finally, here are some tips for kids who want to practice the Law of Attraction:

- Set clear intentions for what you want.
- Break down your goals into achievable steps.
- Believe in yourself and maintain an optimistic attitude.
- Take consistent action towards your goal every day.

With hard work and commitment to achieving your goals through the power of positive thinking, anything is possible. The path ahead may be full of unexpected surprises but don't forget, with resilience and determination, all dreams can become reality!

The end.

On: Trustworthiness

Once upon a time there was a young boy named Bob who lived with his parents in a small town. Bob was always kind and gentle towards others and was known as an honest and trustworthy person by all of his family, friends, and neighbours.

Bob's parents were especially proud of him because he could always be relied upon to tell the truth even when it might not have been easy to do. His parents taught him from a young age the importance of being trustworthy.

They showed him that honesty would always be rewarded in the end, no matter what situation he ended up facing.

Being trustworthy meant that people knew they could count on Bob to do what he said he would do. It also allowed him to make strong bonds with those around him, and much quicker than someone who didn't share this trait. When Bob spoke or promised something, people believed what he said because they knew it came from an honest place.

As Bob got older and grew into adulthood, being trustworthy continued to benefit him greatly. He was able to obtain meaningful work more easily because employers already knew of his reputation for honesty and reliability before hiring him. Additionally, it gave Bob greater confidence as he navigated through life's challenges because he knew that whatever decision or action he chose had been rooted in truthfulness.

On the other hand, not being trustworthy can lead to many negative consequences. People may not view your word as reliable anymore, which can hurt relationships both personally and professionally. When you cannot be trusted, other people start second-guessing your motives rather than assuming you are coming from good intentions. This can make it difficult for them to take you seriously or form any real connection with you in the future.

By understanding the power of being trustworthy, and learning how important it is to stay true to one's word, even when obstacles present themselves, everyone can benefit immensely from keeping their promises, whether big or small.

Trustworthiness builds better relationships among family members, friends, and colleagues alike. It also provides reassurance for those around you that your intentions are pure, no matter what task needs tending to.

But most of all, Bob felt good inside knowing that he chose honesty over dishonesty every day, and it made all the difference in his life!

The end.

On: Visualisation

Once upon a time there was an athlete who had a dream. She dreamed of winning a gold medal at the Olympics. Every day she would take the time to visualise what it would feel like when she reaches her goal. She could see herself crossing the finish line first, and then standing on top of the podium to hear her national anthem.

The athlete was determined to reach her goal and made sure to keep visualising it every day until it became reality. She trained hard, pushing herself beyond what she thought was possible, all in order to focus on making her visualisation a reality.

Little by little, as she progressed in her training, she started believing more and more in her ability and potential. The visualisation of success kept driving her forward, and before long, that is exactly what happened: she won her gold medal!

This example shows how important it is to have a clear vision of your goal if you want to succeed. It's not just about having an idea. it's actually relying on your imagination and seeing yourself achieving that which you hope for. By doing this regularly, you will be able to manifest what you imagine in real life. This also applies to any other goals we wish for, whether that's becoming successful in business, gaining higher grades at school, or even creating great relationships with others.

No matter what our dreams are, approaching them with patience and confidence through visualisation will be key to our success!

The end.

On: Vulnerability

Once upon a time there was a young boy. He was often told he should strive to be strong and confident, and never show his vulnerabilities. Despite this, the little boy was actually quite shy and sensitive.

One day, his teacher set an assignment for the class. This was to go outside and make a friend in the school yard. The little boy was terrified at the thought of it. What if nobody liked him? But he had no choice. He had to go out into the playground.

When he got there, he spotted a girl sitting alone under a tree looking up into its branches. He watched her quietly from afar before hesitantly asking if she wanted to play with him. Surprised, but pleased by his offer, she accepted eagerly.

The two of them began talking about their interests, their families, and the world around them as they built castles made of sand in the schoolyard together. As their conversations grew deeper, the little boy slowly started opening up about things he normally kept hidden — his fears and doubts about himself, about life, and even about friendship itself.

As strange as it may seem, this act of vulnerability is what made him truly brave that day. It made him braver than any attempt to conceal his true self could ever have done. By opening up and showing himself as who he really was, he'd done something far more powerful than simply proving his strength or confidence in front of others.

The girl had also opened up to reveal her true self over the afternoon, so despite never having met each other before that day, they ended up feeling like they knew each other well. They made plans to continue playing together another day, and both went home feeling happy with huge smiles on their faces. It was an unexpected connection made between two strangers!

At that moment, the little boy realised something big. Showing your vulnerabilities can be more courageous than trying to hide them away from everyone else. This is because in doing so, you'll find understanding friends who are

willing to accept you for who you really are.
When you're honest with others (and yourself).
the connections you make can sometimes end up
being more powerful than anything else imaginable!

The end.

The end.

"Children have a natural sense of abundance and feel joy when given the freedom to explore and be creative. Abundance is not just about having a lot of things, but also about feeling rich in experiences and opportunities."

Robert N. Jacobs

Ingram Content Group UK Ltd.
Milton Keynes UK
UKHW050704050623
422881UK00010B/120

9 781803 814728